POPS LOVES YOU

To the Pops who are the
captains of laughter and fun. You
are not just grandpas, you are
grand-masters of joy!

This book belongs to:

_____

From: _____

In a world so big
With skies so blue
Guess who loves you?
Pops! Yes, it's true.

With a smile that
Warms your heart,
Pops is there for you
Right from the start.

So dance around
And clap your hands.
In Pops's love
You'll always stand.

Hide and seek
You laugh and run,
With Pops's love
It's twice the fun.

In Pops's arms
You'll always find
A gentle hug
So sweet and kind.

So hold his hand
And don't let go.
In Pops's love
You'll always grow.

In Pops's love
You'll always find
A shelter strong
A peace of mind.

With every joke
With every jest,
Pops's love
Brings out your best.

So hold his hand
And feel the beat.
In Pops's love
There's no defeat.

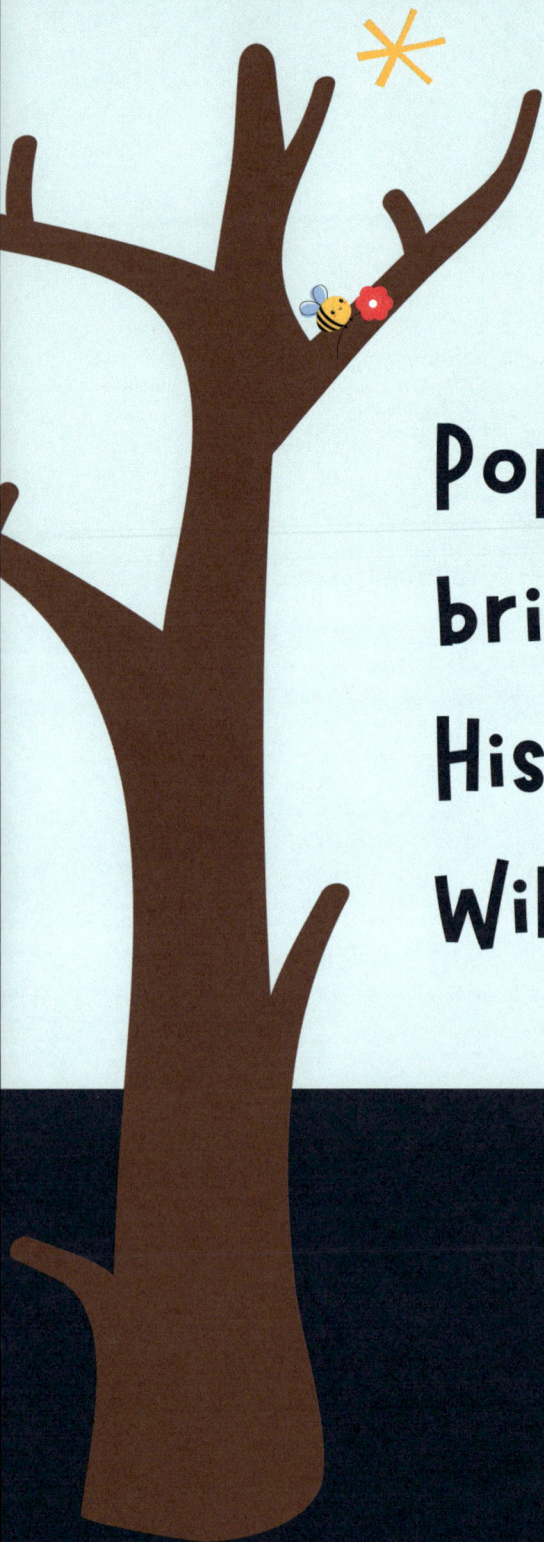

Pops's laughter
brightens up the day.
His love for you
Will never go away.

With every hug
Every snuggle,
Pops's love
Makes your heart juggle.

So laugh out loud
And spread your wings.
In Pops's love
Your heart forever sings.

As you grow each day
In everything you do
Pops's there for you
That is the golden rule.

He'll listen to you
Whatever you say,
Because your words
Brighten his day.

So dance and play
Let your spirit soar.
In Pops's love
You're cherished more.

DID YOU KNOW?

There are hidden bees throughout the book. Read the book again and see if you can find them all.

OTHER BOOKS IN THE 'LOVE YOU' SERIES

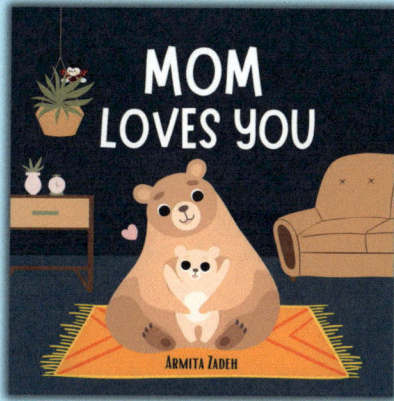

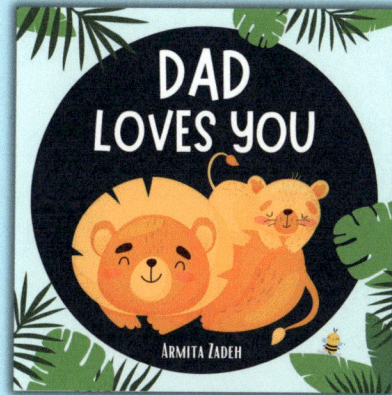

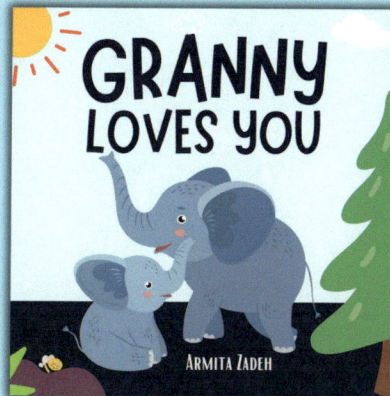

I would love to hear from you if you enjoyed this book. As a self-published author, I read every review and count every star. That's how much each of you means to me.

Made in the USA
Columbia, SC
11 June 2025

59261557R00022